The Nature Kid's Guide to
DOGS

DAVID ANDERSON

For information address LP Media Inc. Publishing,
30012 Variolite St NW, Princeton MN 55371
www.lpmedia.org

Publication Data

Dogs
The Nature Kid's Guide to Dogs — First edition.

Summary: "Learn all about Dogs, the Nature Kid Way"
— Provided by publisher.

ISBN: 979-8-89818-187-1

[1. Dogs - Non-Fiction] I. Title.

Title: The Nature Kid's Guide to Dogs

CONTENTS

DOGS EVERYWHERE

4

Woof! A husky with bright blue eyes trots inside the house.

Dogs have been our best friends for thousands of years. They live on every continent except Antarctica, from tiny villages to big cities.

Many dogs are family pets with cozy beds and warm spots by the fire. But not all dogs live indoors. Some guard sheep and goats on big ranches, sleeping outside with the animals they protect.

In the far north, sled dogs like huskies live in cold, snowy places. Their thick fur keeps them warm far below zero. In the Australian outback, cattle dogs work in the blazing heat all day long.

Wherever dogs call home, they find a way to make life better for the people around them.

WOLF ROOTS

Wolves and dogs can understand each other's howls and body language, even today!

Howl! A German shepherd lifts its head to the moon.

Every dog on Earth, from the tiniest Chihuahua to the biggest Great Dane, came from wolves over 15,000 years ago.

Friendly wolves began hanging around human camps looking for scraps, and people and wolves learned to help each other.

Over time, those wolves became tamer and tamer until they were no longer wild at all.

Some breeds like German shepherds still look a lot like their wolf **ancestors**. Others look nothing like a wolf. But every dog still carries a little bit of wolf inside.

TINY TO TALL

The tallest dog ever was a Great Dane named Zeus. He stood 44 inches tall! He could drink out of the kitchen sink without jumping up!

Bark! A bulldog waddles across the yard on short legs.

Dogs come in all shapes and sizes. A tiny Chihuahua can weigh just four pounds, while a Great Dane can tip the scales at over 150. That is like comparing a house cat to a baby deer!

Medium-sized dogs like bulldogs and beagles are some of the most popular.

Labrador retrievers are a little bigger, weighing up to 80 pounds, and have been America's favorite **breed** for years.

No matter the size, every dog thinks it belongs on your lap.

PAWS AND PARTS

Dogs have three eyelids! The third one helps keep their eyes moist and clean.

Sniff! A beagle presses its nose to the ground. It follows an exciting smell.

Dogs are built for action. Their soft paw pads work like sneakers, protecting their feet from hot pavement and icy ground. Strong claws help them dig, grip, and scramble over rough terrain.

Their coats come in every style. Poodles have curly fur that never stops growing. Bulldogs have short, smooth coats. Beagles have long, floppy ears that sweep scents toward their noses like tiny brooms.

And that wagging tail? It is like a mood ring. Fast wag means happy. Slow wag means unsure. Tucked tail means scared.

SUPER SNIFFERS

Growl! A beagle sniffs along a garden path. Its nose wiggles with joy.

A dog's nose is its superpower. Dogs have up to 300 million **scent sensors** in their noses. People only have 6 million! That is why dogs can smell things we never could.

Beagles are some of the best sniffers around. Their long, floppy ears help sweep scents toward their noses with every step.

Dogs hear really well too. They can hear sounds four times farther away than people can. That is why your dog knows someone is at the door long before you do.

SO MANY SHAPES

Thump! A bulldog plops down on a soft pillow. Time for a nap!

There are around 400 different dog breeds in the world. Each breed has a unique look and traits!

Bulldogs have wrinkly faces and pushed-in noses. They are calm and love to relax indoors. Huskies have thick fur and blue or brown eyes. Their coats help them stay warm in cold places.

Dalmatians have white coats with black dots. These spotted dogs once ran beside fire wagons!

DID YOU KNOW?

The Basenji is called the barkless dog. It yodels instead of barking!

DINNERTIME

Munch! A hungry Labrador puppy chomps kibble from its bowl.

Dogs need good food to stay healthy. Most dogs eat dry kibble or wet food made just for them.

Labradors love to eat! They need measured **portions** so they do not get too heavy. Dalmatians need special food to keep their kidneys healthy.

Some foods are dangerous for dogs. Chocolate, grapes, and onions can make them very sick. Always ask a grown-up before giving your dog a new treat.

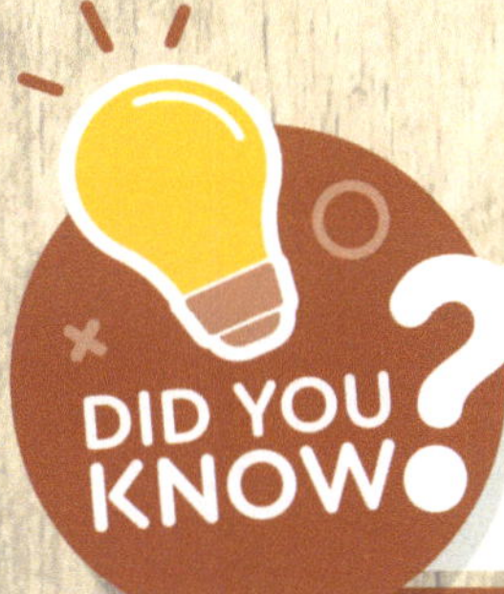

Dogs have about 1,700 taste buds. Humans have 9,000!

SMART PUPS

FUN FACT!
Dogs learn hand signals better than words! Some dogs can learn over 100 commands.

Swoosh! A golden retriever runs to its owner with a ball.

Dogs are fast learners. With practice, most dogs can learn to follow commands, do tricks, and even take on real jobs.

Golden retrievers love to please, which makes them easy to train. German shepherds are quick learners too. Police and rescue teams count on them to track down missing people and keep communities safe.

Training works best with treats and short lessons. Say a word like "sit," and when your dog does it, reward them right away. Dogs learn fast when training feels like a game!

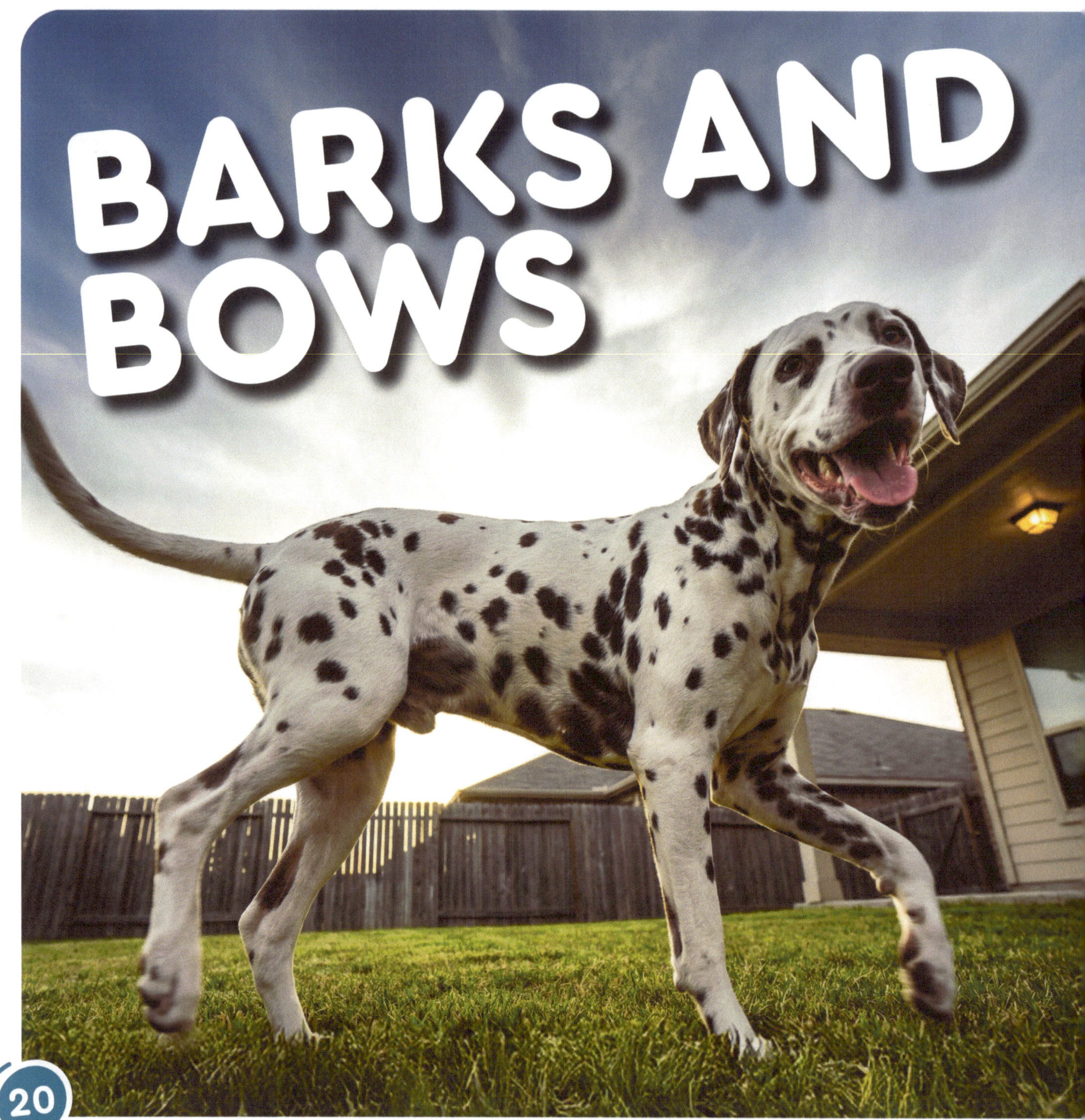

BARKS AND BOWS
20

Yip! A dalmatian wags its spotted tail at its owner.

Dogs talk without using words. They use their bodies and voices to show how they feel!

A wagging tail shows excitement, but it does not always mean a dog is happy. A tucked tail means the dog is scared. Ears that point forward show interest. Flat ears can mean fear.

Different barks mean different things. A high bark might mean excitement. A low growl is a warning.

Dogs use 23 face muscles in their ears, eyes, and mouth to show feelings!

FETCH FUN

Zoom! A husky races across the yard toward a rope toy.

Dogs need playtime every day. Play keeps their bodies strong and their minds sharp!

Some dogs need extra exercise. Huskies love to run and pull. A tired husky is a happy husky! Labradors and Border Collies love to play too. They will chase balls or catch frisbees for hours.

Tug-of-war is fun for many dogs. Puzzle toys are great too. They exercise a dog's body and mind!

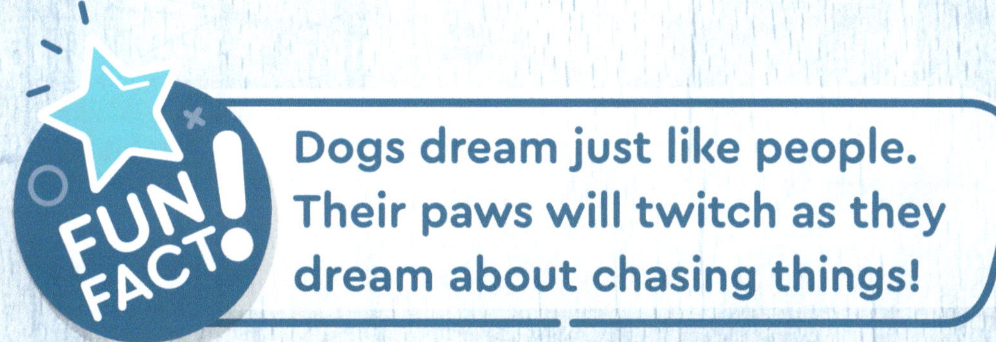

ZOOM ZOOMIES

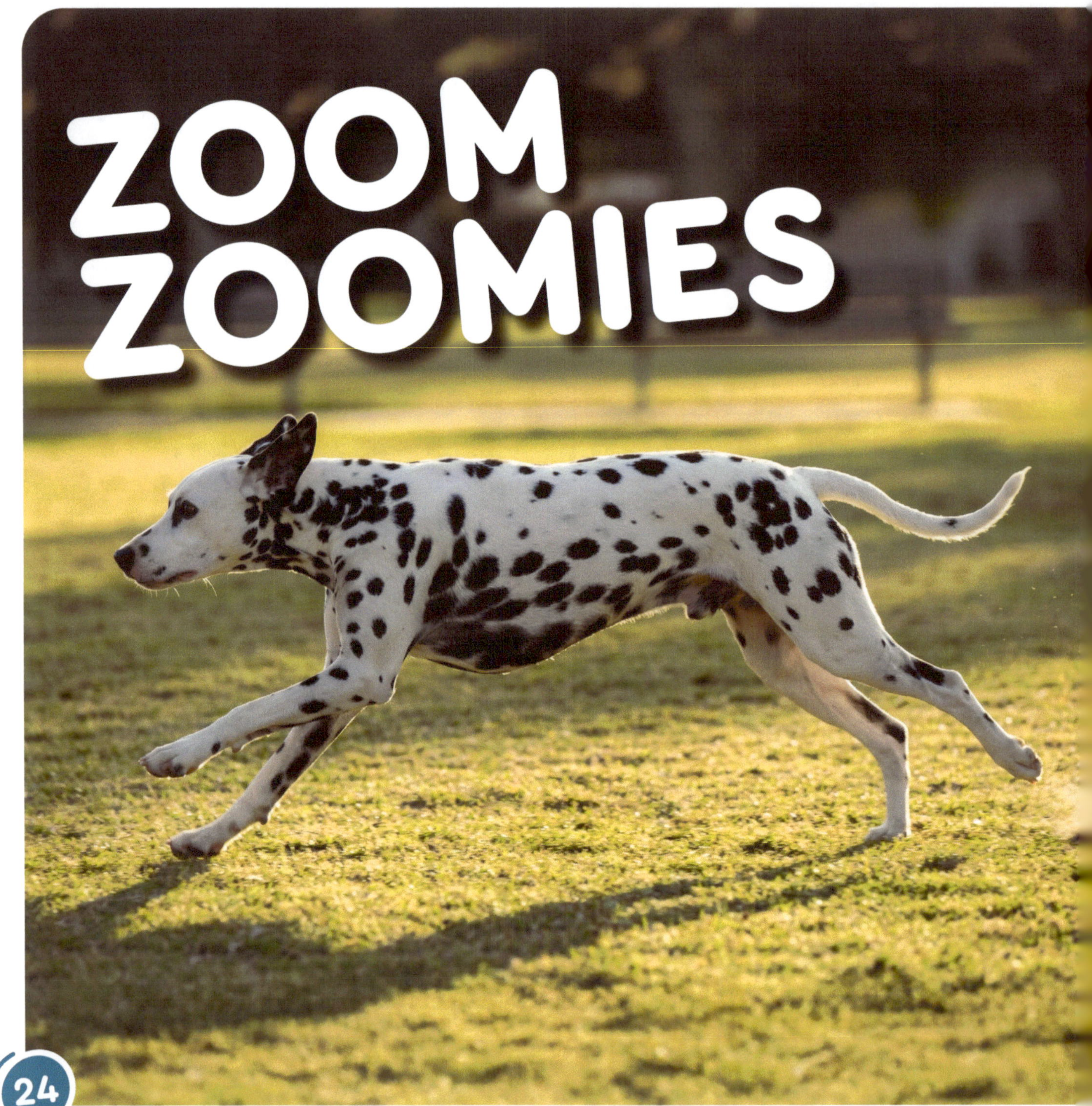

Whoosh! A dalmatian sprints across the park. Watch it go!

Dogs move in many cool ways. They run, jump, climb, and swim!

Dalmatians are fast runners. They can run for miles without getting tired. But they aren't the fastest dog. Greyhounds can run up to 45 miles per hour!

Beagles trot with their noses down, following scents. Many dogs are great swimmers. Newfoundland dogs even have webbed feet to help them swim!

A greyhound can go from standing still to 30 miles per hour in just three seconds!

25

NAP TIME

DID YOU KNOW?

Dogs curl up in a ball to protect their bellies and stay warm while they sleep.

Yawn! A fluffy poodle stretches after a cozy nap. Time to play!

Dogs sleep a lot! Most adult dogs snooze for 12 to 14 hours a day. Puppies need even more rest, sometimes sleeping up to 20 hours.

Dogs do not sleep all at once like people do. They take short naps throughout the day and wake up ready to play at a moment's notice. That is because dogs are light sleepers, always listening for something exciting.

Big, heavy breeds like bulldogs and mastiffs nap the most. Bulldogs are famous for snoring so loud you can hear them from across the room!

PACK PALS

FUN FACT!
Dogs can tell friendly dogs from unfriendly ones just by sniffing them for a few seconds!

Pant! A German shepherd plays with two other dogs.

Dogs are pack animals at heart. They love being part of a group, whether that means a family of people, a house full of pets, or a team of working dogs pulling a sled together.

German shepherds bond closely with their families and will guard them with fierce loyalty.

Huskies love company so much that they can howl and cry when left alone too long.

Some dogs are happiest with a furry friend by their side. Others want all the attention for themselves.

Every dog has its own personality!

PUPPY TIME

Puppies are born without teeth! Their baby teeth start coming in at three weeks old.

Snuggle! A curly poodle lies down with her new puppies.

A mother dog carries her puppies for about two months before they are born. Most litters have four to six puppies, but Dalmatians can have 10 to 15 at once!

Newborn puppies are tiny, blind, and helpless. They cannot see or hear for the first two weeks and spend almost all their time sleeping and eating.

Around four weeks old, puppies start to change. They learn to eat solid food. They start walking and playing. **Breeders** keep a close eye on all the puppies to make sure they grow strong and healthy.

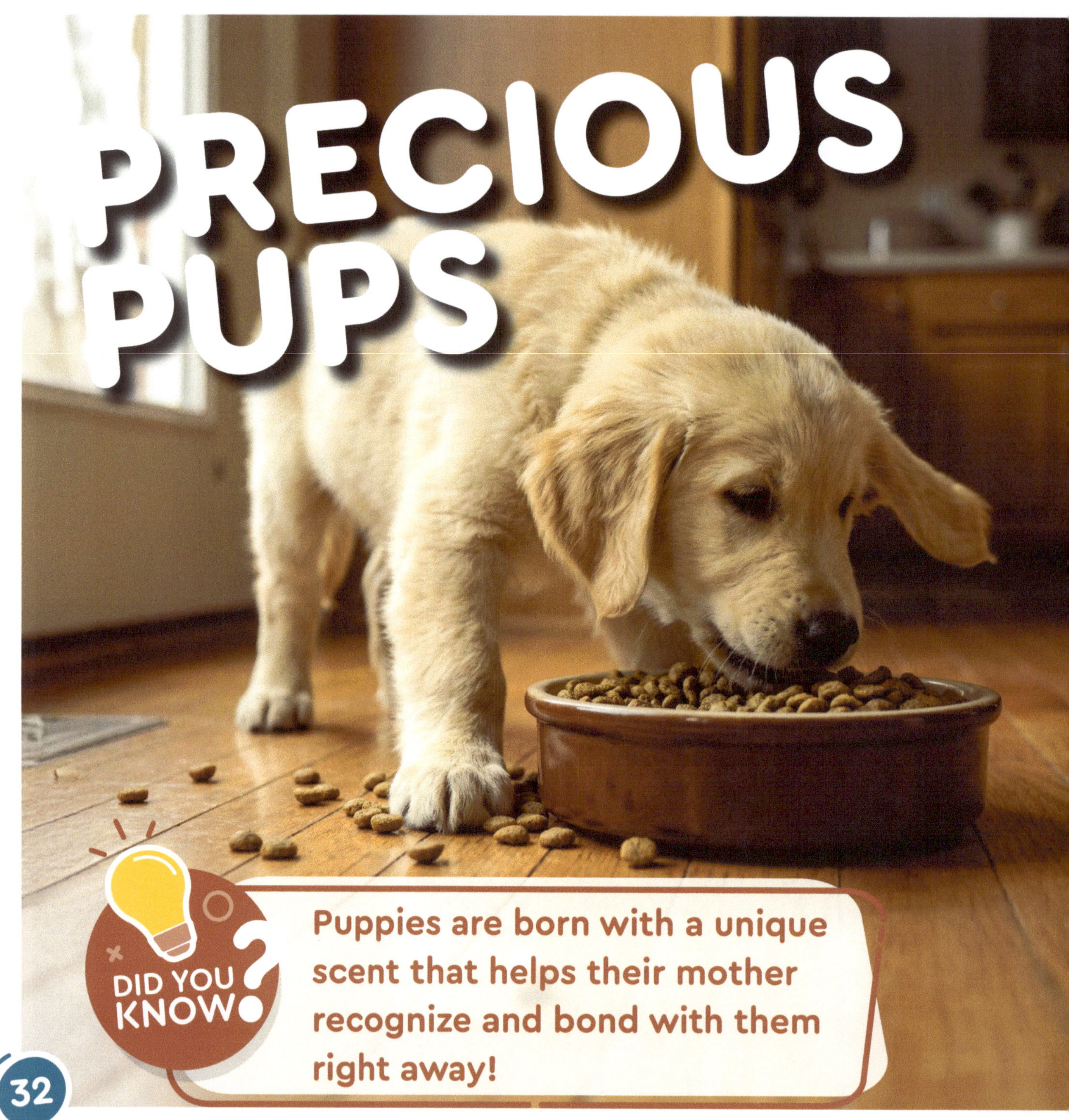

PRECIOUS PUPS

Crunch! A Golden retriever puppy munches on his kibble.

From four to eight weeks old, puppies change fast. They wrestle with their brothers and sisters, learning how to play without biting too hard. Their mother teaches them manners that will help them become good dogs later on.

By eight weeks old, puppies are running, tumbling, and getting into everything. They can eat on their own and are curious about the whole world around them.

Between eight and twelve weeks, most puppies are ready to leave their mother and go to their new families.

GROWING UP

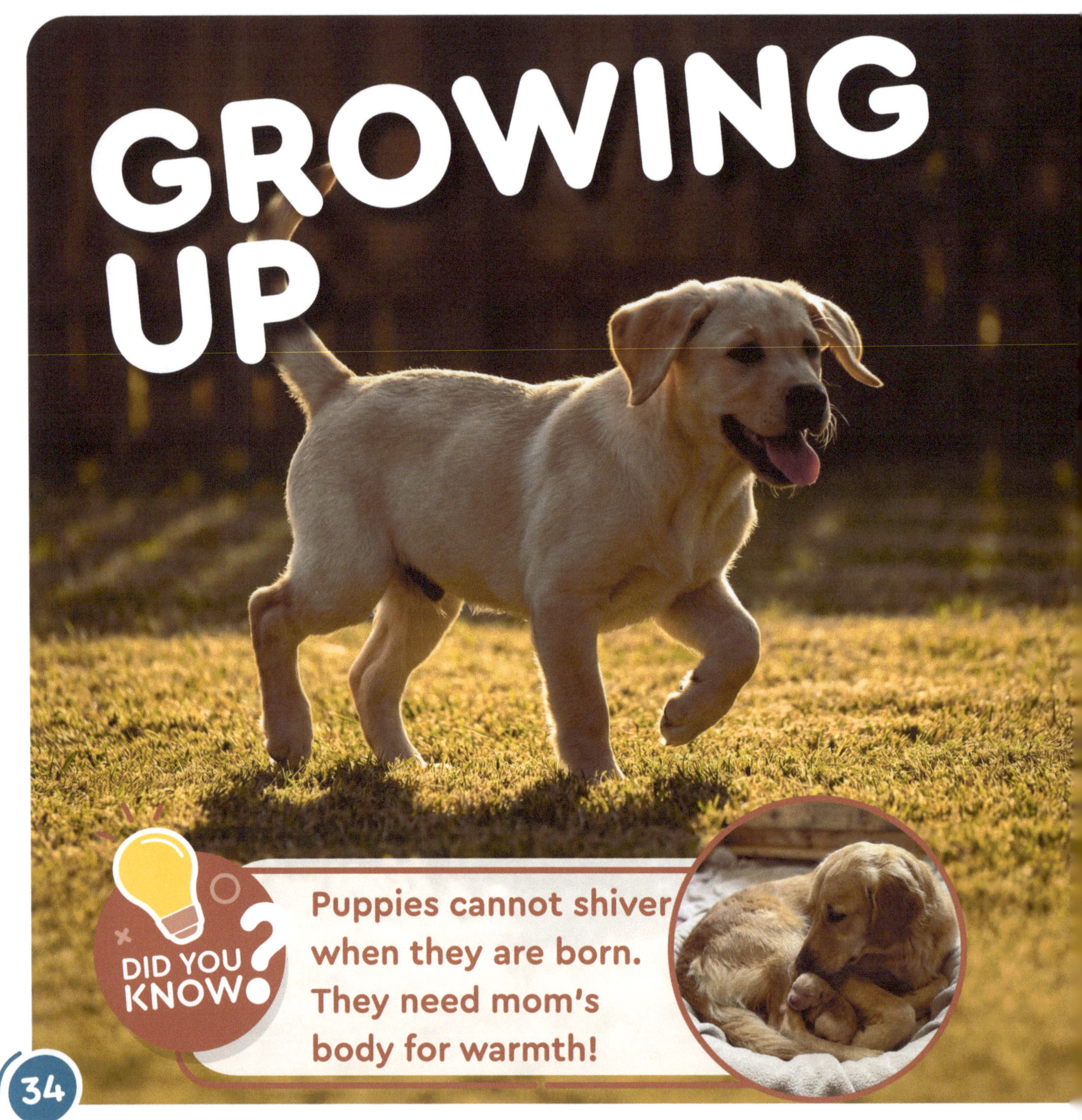

Puppies cannot shiver when they are born. They need mom's body for warmth!

Woof! A Labrador Retriever greets its owner with a wagging tail.

When a puppy arrives at its new home, everything is an adventure. New smells, new sounds, and new people! The first few weeks are about getting comfortable and learning the rules.

From three to six months old, puppies grow fast. They lose their baby teeth, learn basic commands, and have more energy than they know what to do with.

Most small breeds are fully grown by their first birthday. But large breeds like Great Danes keep growing until they are two or three years old!

SUPER PUPS

DID YOU KNOW?
Dogs may sense earthquakes before humans feel them! They can feel tiny ground vibrations we cannot detect.

Woof! A search and rescue dog helps search for a lost hiker.

Some dogs have jobs that save lives. Search and rescue dogs sniff through earthquake rubble, deep snow, and thick forests to find people who are lost or trapped.

Labrador retrievers work as guide dogs, leading people who cannot see safely through busy streets. These smart dogs learn over 100 commands.

Malinois often work with soldiers and police, sniffing out hidden dangers. Some can even smell diseases before a doctor can find them. Dogs truly are heroes with four legs and a wagging tail.

FOREVER FRIENDS

Wag! A wiggly Beagle puppy jumps up to say hello to its favorite person.

There is nothing like coming home to a dog. Their tail wags. They spin around. They are so happy just to see you!

Dogs do not care what you look like or how old you are. They just want to be near you and spend time playing together.

Whether your best friend is a giant Great Dane or a tiny Goldendoodle, every dog has one thing in common. They give you their whole heart, and all they ask for is a little love and maybe a belly rub.

GLOSSARY

ancestors
Family members who lived a very long time ago.

breeds
Different types of dogs that look and act in special ways.

scent sensors
Tiny parts inside a nose that help smell things.

portions
The amount of food you give at one time.

breeders
A person who carefully pairs dogs together so they can have healthy puppies.